INTUITION IS YOUR SUPERPOWER

LEARN HOW TO FOLLOW YOUR GUT AND GAIN CONFIDENCE IN THE LITTLE VOICE AT THE BACK OF YOUR MIND

BY BERNADETTE BALLA

TABLE OF CONTENTS

ABOUT THE AUTHOR

For the longest time, from my adolescence to my early thirties, I was struggling to find my life purpose. I didn't know what it was, or how I could find it.

BERNADETTE BALLA

During my pivotal growing-up years, my father abandoned our family. And I never understood why. After that, I felt helpless and empty all the time. I was paralyzed by fear: I had questions, but no answers. I knew I had problems, but I had no solutions. My self-esteem plunged. I didn't know how to fix myself, and I was cynical about my future.

Unbeknownst to me, my father's leaving planted in me a deep fear of abandonment that shaped all my future relationships: with friends, with the men I dated, and most of all, with myself. It would start from something seemingly trivial, like whenever I texted a friend and she didn't reply within an hour or two, I would grow antsy. *Why hasn't she replied? Is she avoiding me? Did I say something to annoy her previously? Am I about to lose this friend? What the hell?* I was so damn afraid of saying anything that might sound potentially critical that I held my tongue many times. I wasn't able to say what I truly felt. I couldn't commit to totally truthful relationships because I was worried my friends might cut me off. That they would leave me, like he did.

For nearly two decades I woke up with dread hitting my gut every day, and no drugs, no partner, and no amount of money could bring me peace during this period of deep gloom.

Until, in 2015, I officially hit rock bottom.

I had been in a toxic five-year relationship with someone who couldn't emotionally connect. He didn't know how to express or establish intimacy and was very insensitive to how his actions hurt me. Our relationship made me feel even more isolated, many things were bottled up.

My job didn't satisfy me, either—working in Silicon Valley made me feel my connections were transactional and lacked authenticity. The company I was working for had been purchased for one billion dollars—so, big yay, I should have been jumping for joy...

But the truth is, I felt lost and empty. I couldn't see anything in my life near "Happy" or "Optimistic." Nothing made me feel *alive*!

An Unexpected Connection

In the thick of my darkness, I felt inevitably drawn towards research on happiness, and it seemed that everywhere I turned I kept hearing about the benefits of meditation, and how it could bring us inner calm and happiness. So I tried it.

What I didn't expect was that it also engaged me with my intuition. My inner compass, which steered me towards a path I'm meant for. My inner voice, which helped me tap into a wealth of wisdom, into answers I already had within me.

One by one, my doubts started to clear up—things began to make sense. Three years into my journey, I understand that only I, Bernadette Balla, can create my own positive transformation. That only I can find and determine my true meaning in life.

And that became my life purpose.

MY MISSION

Writing this book is my way of reaching out to all the younger Bernadettes, people who feel lost and want to be found again—through their own intuitive power.

What you probably don't realize is that everything you know about your life so far, you've learned from your parents and the society. But you haven't learned much from the person who matters the most—yourself.

Your intuition can make you feel more secure in your life, and it can guide you to make WAY better decisions. You need to understand how it works so you can learn to trust it.

And this is what I'm here for. I'm here to tell you more about your intuition. I'm here to help you learn to trust it so you can make the right decisions for that future you deserve. Through my stories and life learnings, I want to empower you to find your inner connection, so you can find your inner power.

You can connect with me on:

Instagram: www.instagram.com/bernadetteballa

YouTube: https://www.youtube.com/c/BernadettesGuidetoSpirituality

Facebook: www.facebook.com/whoisbernadette

CHAPTER ONE

HOW MY BODY TOLD ME THE STORY I'VE BEEN TRYING TO FORGET

I t was a winter's night filled with sounds. As I climbed into bed, I heard the rain pitter-patter on the streets of San Francisco outside. *"It's Beginning to Look a Lot Like Christmas"* had been playing on repeat in my head the whole day and looked set to accompany me to sleep.

Not a care in the world! I was happy. When suddenly, the booming became *too* loud, *too* near. I woke up and heard footsteps and banging rattling through my paper-thin walls. It was my neighbor. Drunk, again.

For about an hour and a half, I heard him talking loudly. His TV was blaring, and more footsteps thudded past my apartment towards his. Dammit, he was having a party!

"Give him another hour", I told myself.

The noise went on and on and I couldn't get back to sleep—my brain remained active to the sounds, and even when I closed my eyes I was still aware of everything that was going on. I felt my skin crawl, while my mind and heart were racing.

What was causing me, a 36-year-old woman, to be this triggered by a neighbor who had no idea he was setting off all kinds of trauma in me? Why did I feel so vulnerable and helpless?

"Urgh, why can't I be one of those people who could sleep through anything?"

I grabbed my pillow and automatically crawled into a fetal position, unable to control my anxiety. And when morning came and I had to drag myself to work, I felt exhausted and mentally drained.

For years I was trying to figure out why middle-of-the-night noises always gave me so much stress. But a few weeks after my neighbor's not-so-neighborly episode, I finally understood.

My big WHY!

That moment of insight came to me in a pretty strange way at first, but then it turned into the most freeing experience ever. I'll tell you all about it in a minute.

My Spiritual Journey Involves a Hamster Wheel

In part, this book is about questions. I've been on a spiritual awakening journey since 2015. Spirituality is like an intelligent higher power that starts with loving yourself. It's basically self-discovery.

There was so much talk about the benefits of meditation—It was difficult at first. I couldn't concentrate that well and kept drifting off. So I told myself, *"Meditate for only one minute. Just breathe in and out."*

Soon, that one minute progressed to two. By and by, it lasted longer, one minute at a time.

Meditation is powerful : it has brought me deeply profound revelations about my mind and thoughts. However, at that point, I still found myself repeating certain negative patterns of behaviour—like a hamster on its wheel, I was part of my own insane loop going round and round.

Meditation made me aware that I had to get off that wheel, but I was not ready yet. It was a lot easier clinging on than getting off. Besides, I didn't know how to get off exactly, so I carried on without doing anything about it.

I continued meditating every day, and I must have progressed deeper into it unknowingly, because one day, in a deep meditative state, I found myself astral-traveling.

Astral what?

Astral travel, or astral projection, is a sort of out-of-body experience where your consciousness is able to leave your physical body and travel (like a really cool Doctor Strange superpower). My spiritual journey accelerated after that. I began having experiences of traveling back in time to seemingly random points in my life through meditation.

Yes, key phrase—"seemingly random." But of course, they were not random. They were usually unpleasant memories lodged in the shadows of my mind. Memories that have been waiting for me for decades.

And now that I'm looking at my past and my present issues, the question is: What can I do to *understand* them? How can I figure out why I feel what I feel?

I have memories that have been waiting for me to seek them out again so I can understand them better. Or at least attempt to understand them better. The only way I could do this is by getting in touch with my intuition.

Here's the Rest of My Story

After several years of practicing meditation, there have been some occasions when I experienced time travel. During one of these sessions, I astral-traveled back to my childhood home, back to the room I had as a teenager, which was right next to my parent's room.

As I stepped in, I immediately understood that my anxiety had actually begun many, many years ago. In that very room.

"Holy shit", I said to myself.

It recalled the same feelings I'd experienced when my next-door neighbor woke me up.

The feeling of anxiousness.

The feeling of dread.

The feeling of being helpless.

My father.

He would tell me that there was no point in studying and going to school because, according to him, I'd grow up to become a prostitute. He frequently came home vomiting on the bed he shared with my mom. She would have to clean it up. He would burp and hiccup. It was horrible—the hurled abuse. Those little noises at night.

The sounds were secretly stashed inside me. My neighbor's episode brought them out again and I was reliving those scary times from my childhood. No wonder I couldn't fall back asleep!

Noises were my trigger. In times of anxiety, my own body would respond in this following way: I would feel my stomach churning and hear the rumbling sound it makes. I would hug my stomach, rock back and forth, and tap my restless feet on the ground. A feeling of dread would rush through, and I'd know that the day ahead would be a hard one.

For other people, the rumbling noise in their stomach tells them food is being digested. But for me, it's a warning that something is not well. It's a sign to distance myself from a situation that is not serving me. It's a sign of *"Watch out and pay attention"* and I always listen to it.

What You Can Get from This Book

The reason I wrote this book is that I want to encourage you to access your intuition more—use it to help yourself understand and discover your inner and outer world, and the relationship between the two.

In this book, you will:

- Learn what your body is trying to tell you through your aches and pain. Our bodies are constantly trying to send us messages. In Chapter 2, you will learn the basic Body Wisdom interpretations. Find out what the tightness in your chest could be about.

- Pick up practical and interesting exercises to help you connect with your intuition. Nope, meditation is not one of them. Expect these creative exercises in Chapter 7.

- Take a quiz at the end of this book to see how intuitive you really are. This will be fun, I promise!

And more.

You might not find all your answers at once—in fact, you might add even more questions as you move forward. Here's the strangely satisfying part: It will be worth it.

You will get more curious about yourself and find important answers along the way.

You will not be stressed out when you don't have the answers right away.

You will grow to be a bigger and more confident person on the inside.

CHAPTER TWO

YOUR BODY IS INTUITIVE

You may not know this, but your body is able to store memories of incidents from the past in different areas. Turns out, our brain isn't the only place that holds our memories—other parts of our bodies are pretty good at it, too!

But what exactly are body memories? Well, they could be a smell, or a touch, or, like in my case, a sound. And our bodies can remember both good and bad times.

For example, have you ever caught the scent of cinnamon and immediately felt safe and happy? Perhaps your body remembers the time you were seven and you visited your granny who was baking you cinnamon rolls—it was a safe and happy time, and your body kept that memory. Through the sweetness of cinnamon, which is the trigger, you can feel what you felt at that time.

Body memories are amazing. They can affect the way you move, think, feel, and even the way you behave. They know your past hurts, they know your current insecurities. They know what you're worried about and what you fear.

What My Hips Told Me

I have tight hips. I feel an uncomfortable tension in my pelvic area every day. Whenever I walk, climb the stairs, or even curl up in bed, I'd feel aches and soreness in my hips.

One day, while mindlessly scrolling through my phone, I came across a book by Bessel van der Kolk, M.D. called "The Body Keeps the Score: Brain, Mind, and Body in the Healing of Trauma." Through that unexpected encounter, I began learning about body wisdom. I used all my learnings to boost healing in my mind, body, and spirit. The body wisdom theory taught me to understand my body on a deeper level.

As it turned out, the tightness in my hips was related to my deep sense of insecurity. Hips are where we store our unprocessed emotions and repressed issues that stress us out. On the surface, I appeared like I had my life together, but truth be told, even with a good job, a roof over my head, I didn't feel alive. I didn't feel fulfilled.

I didn't know who I was.

Now that I've started to understand what my body is telling me, I'm paying attention to what I need, I feel like I've gained access to the secret of the Universe.

I feel secure despite the times of loneliness and other matters.

I know that the only person who can break me is me.

It's shocking how clearly our bodies know our inner fears, so much more than our minds do.

Ignorance ISN'T Bliss

Many years ago, when I experienced my first huge emotional breakdown, I also broke my left foot. The entire left side of my body was numb. It took more than a year to heal and till this day, it still isn't right.

I brushed the numbness off and carried on with my life.

Physically, I was cleared. What I chose to ignore was finding out the spiritual significance of that injury. Had

I found out more about body wisdom and root chakra, I would have learned that my emotional foundation was out of whack. That I was living in constant fear and anxiety about my basic needs.

By thinking of my numbness as nothing more than a distraction, I failed to address my deep insecurities and sense of unworthiness.

I guess this is why when I had my second breakdown right after I quit my Silicon Valley job (to work on my spirituality creatively), my body decided to make me face my insecurities with a bigger WHAM.

As I'm writing this, I'm recuperating from a condition that got me admitted to the emergency room three times within the last 3 weeks, flown between LA and San Francisco, through at least 10 doctors and numerous nurses, painful IV drips, and countless rounds of morphine, Reglan, Compazine, Lorazepam, Prozac, and painkillers.

The doctors couldn't explain what was happening to me. Others told me it was "food poisoning," "just a virus." My gut told me something else: That it had to do with my brain-stomach connection.

So one afternoon, before I was transported to the third ER, I called up a private doctor. Dr. John came to my house because I keep throwing up till I pass out, it was dangerous. I asked him if this was a brain-stomach connection thing. Cyclic Vomiting Syndrome.

"Maybe," he said. He asked me where it hurt.

"My throat, jaws, the whole neck, and lungs."

BAM. Right then, I knew. My pain was all located in the throat chakra, the passageway of speaking your truth and communicating that with others. And it all made sense.

I Was Afraid

Of how others would judge my book and my spiritual entrepreneurship. There had been nights when I felt creatively debilitated because I worried about telling people that I connect with a higher power. I was scared of not having the vocabulary to make others understand. I was anxious about how my ex-colleagues in Silicon Valley would react.

This ridiculous illness has been a wake-up call to address my insecurities. No more brushing it aside!

So I've turned to writing down my dreams and drawing tarot cards (techniques and logic explained in Chapter Seven) to learn what my intuition wants me to know at this stage.

In one of my dreams, a young girl followed me blindly through the woods because she wanted to find out what I was teaching. In another, I was yelling like a drama queen because nobody heard what I was saying. In yet another, I saw a house that was close to a giant beach, and a huge wave rolled up to swallow it.

What are my dreams telling me? That I'm worried about being heard. But also, that there might be others out there who need me to guide them out of the woods.

(Tip: If you want to remember your dreams, drink lots of water so you will need to wake up in the middle of the night to pee. Before peeing, quickly write or audio-record what you can recall about your dream. It will be vivid because you've been waken during Rapid Eye Movement.)

My tarot card readings have given me stronger and happier affirmations that I am on the right path. Page of pentacles, Queen of pentacles, Eight of Wands. They are providing me with love and support while guiding me towards a life of ideas and creativity.

How This Works for You

When you are feeling unwell and nobody can tell you what the matter is, give more attention to what your body is telling you. Listen to your intuition. Maybe it is a virus. Maybe you ate the wrong thing. Maybe it is something deeper in your emotions. Note where it hurts and check out the body wisdom chart (given below in this chapter).

Whatever you do, do NOT ignore it.

During both my breakdowns, my chakras were speaking to me. I was blinded by the logical world and chose to ignore them. Each part of your body has a story to tell. Sit down and listen.

As physically painful as this whole episode has been, I also feel that this experience is a gift. How else would I have known that I've actually been so afraid of being judged as a spiritual person?

Now You

If you want to identify where your negative body memories are stored, simply find the areas in your body that are inflexible, tight, or just somewhere that's bothering you. This is a huge step towards healing. And it's a perfect way to start noticing what your body has been trying to tell you.

Perhaps you've been feeling a little lost about where you are in life? Perhaps you feel insecure about your relationships and don't know what to do?

Breathe deep. Relax. And listen to your body. It's trying to tell you the stuff you need to hear.

Body Wisdom Chart

Here's a chart/diagram for you to refer to:

- **Forehead:** Where we convey our intellect.

- **Brows:** Our intuitive centre; Where we communicate our emotions.

- **Nose:** Linked to our heart and smell; Our self-recognition; How we respond sexually.

- **Mouth:** Linked with how we nourish ourselves; A sense of security and willingness to welcome new ideas; Survivorship.

- **Jaws:** Tight jaws indicate difficulty in communication; Fear of expressing yourself fully.

- **Throat:** Communication. Do you often hold back from telling the truth about how you feel?

- **Neck:** Where our feelings and thoughts meet; Aches and stiffness can be due to holding things back.

- **Shoulders:** Weight on our shoulders represents our responsibilities. Linked with our daily stress and tension; Lack of self-care.

- **Chest:** Love and relationship issues; Difficulty in breathing deeply can also be due to lack of self-esteem, suppressed feelings, and a sense of being overpowered.

- **Back:** Stored resentment and fears; Where unconscious emotions dwell; Anxiety due to lack of financial support.

- **Upper back:** Stored frustrations; emotional insecurity.

- **Hips:** Unprocessed emotions are stored here; Issues you don't want to deal with.

Check in with yourself regularly during your morning stretches. Is there a strain in your shoulders? Does your lower back ache? How about your jaws? Your chest?

After identifying where tension lies, you can start asking deeper questions like *What regrets am I holding on to? Which area of my life (work, relationship, health etc.) am I worried about? What are my fears and insecurities?*

Use your body wisdom to guide you. Try it!

CHAPTER THREE

YOUR INTUITION IS YOUR SUPERPOWER

So what exactly is intuition?

Some call it their sixth sense, some call it a gut feeling or a hunch. Others call it their inner compass or inner GPS. To me, it's that quiet assertive voice in my head nudging me whether or not I should do something.

It's our capacity to access knowledge and understand things without rationality, without being analytical. It's a form of personal superpower. Something that exists in you and can get stronger if you train it.

And if you allow it.

Your intuition superpower can only shine through and save your day if you choose to pay attention to it.

Unfortunately, most of us tend to dismiss our intuition because we don't want to sound "weird" or because we don't know how to explain it. We often choose not to say anything or go along with what others suggest, in order to avoid any awkwardness.

In other cases, we often confuse intuitive feelings with anxiety, fear, and wishful thinking. I mean, there are so many thoughts in our head! Which one are we going to listen to?

Let me help you clarify this.

Intuition vs. anxiety

It's just another day – you're there, doing your thing and suddenly, you feel something's *off*.

You can't put your finger to it – you start to overthink.

Is something bad going to happen? Are your loved ones okay?

Whatever you do, you can't shake off this feeling. You start to believe your intuition is screaming to you. Damn, what is your gut trying to tell you *so hard*?

And then, as you make it home safely, it dawns on you: that wasn't your gut talking. Nothing bad is going to happen. That's just anxiety!

But how can you tell the two apart? How do you know whenever you have to listen to your gut – or completely ignore the chatter in your head? Learn the difference between intuition and anxiety.

Why do we confuse our gut feeling with anxiety?

People confuse the two because honestly, they sound almost identical. You know, they *sound* the same in your head.

You recognize them as the same – well, at least that's what your rational mind does. But they don't feel the same.

Notice the keyword there: *feel.*

You need to look at how that inner voice makes you feel to be able to distinguish between the two.

Intuition never feels scary – there are no feelings of panic coming with it. Intuition is always calm, assertive, and reassuring.

Anxiety makes it harder to hear your inner voice.

But you can give your inner voice some clarity – even if you're fighting with anxiety.

Here are some tips to help you:

1) Find the pattern

Anxiety usually comes with a pattern.

Something triggers you – and you get upset.

For example, you know how some people get anxious on Sunday – while others get panic attacks before major meetings?

It's your job to be aware of that pattern. Discover your main triggers – maybe it's your boss, maybe it's your ex-boyfriend, maybe it's your mom. Don't obsess about it – just be aware of your emotional triggers.

Whenever you get drowned in worrying, check – are you sweating over one of your usual triggers? If the answer is yes, you may want to cut your intuition some slack – it's not talking to you right now.

2) Do a reality check

Intuition means you're able to fuse together past experiences & real-life knowledge with present-day emotions.

So, do exactly that – use your rational mind to calm down. Do a reality check.

Talk to someone if you need to – preferably someone you trust. Once you say what you've been worrying about out loud, you'll instantly know whether it's been real gut talk or another panic attack.

3) Confusion means one thing only

Are you feeling confused after making a big decision? 99.9% of the time, confusion means only one thing – anxiety.

Intuition never leaves you questioning – you *always* know. You're always at peace with your decision.

4) Watch the intensity of what you experience

Have you noticed how *loud* it gets in your head whenever you're hit by anxiety? Well, anxiety is loud and pushy and generally unpleasant – it just totally overwhelms you.

On the other hand, intuition is more peaceful, soothing. I always describe intuition like a hug – whenever it talks to me, I get the same warm feeling I get from a hug.

Oh, and intuition is never about the past or the future – it's always about the present. Right here, and right now.

If you experience any extreme worry about what had been or what is going to come, then that's not your gut – it's anxiety trying to play tricks on you!

Intuition vs. fear – which one is it?

- ## Intuition is always about the present

Fear often drives you to act based on past trauma or future anxieties. On the other side, your intuition is *always* offering guidance about a *present* moment.

For example – this is an extreme example so you get the point – imagine you're walking back home.

You suddenly decide to make a turn and grab a warm latte in the Starbucks you're passing by. And you don't even drink latte to begin with! Five minutes later, a car comes crashing on the sidewalk – exactly on the same spot where you were moments ago!

- ## Intuition is never limiting

Fear is conditional – *if you don't do that, then this happens.*

However, intuition is never restricting. It's more like a sensation, an idea – some sudden knowledge about something you can't yet see.

Intuition won't say to you – *if you don't move, a car will come crashing onto you!* You simply get an impulse that you act upon – and it may even save your life.

- ## Intuition is always kind

Fear is cruel – and has a way of making you judge yourself. Intuition never judges – it simply guides you.

Intuitive feelings are kind and reassuring, making you feel safe. The message you get is always clear but never loud and nagging.

- **Intuition never feels heavy**

People often describe fear as *heavy* and demanding.

On the other side, intuition feels... definite but liberating. Most of the time, intuition won't even have a specific emotion tied to it.

It'll show up as a sensation of knowing and understanding – even if you rationally can't explain what that knowledge is.

A lot of people fear listening to their intuition, mainly, because they are not familiar with how it feels like. By the end of this chapter, you will have a better understanding of how your intuition communicates. You won't be so fearful to tap into your gut whenever you hear a strong calling for it.

I listen to my gut or intuition closely

CHAPTER FOUR

SIGNS FROM A UNIVERSE CALLED "YOU"

Tapping into our intuition can help us discover how we truly feel and what we want to do next in social settings. Like when you're choosing a new apartment, or when you're at a job interview trying to decide if the company culture is a good fit for you.

Usually, your gut feeling can tell you if the "vibe" of a person, place, or task is positive or negative.

Signs of "Yes, This Is Going to Work Out"

- You start to breathe easier, i.e. your lungs and ribcage area expand well and there is no choking feeling in your throat.

- Your gut isn't nervous—it's calm and settled.

- When you feel a sense of brightness wash over you and you begin to smile. (This tends to happen when you step into a place, like a new apartment, and you just feel "right.")

- When there's a nice, familiar feeling, like a deja vu. It's as if you've met this person before or known him/her for ages.

- Your body leans forward instead of back—this means you're interested in learning more, and it's usually a good sign that this project/task/person is going to help you grow.

- When a handshake or a hug feels cosy, warm, or safe.

- When your heart feels like it's growing slightly bigger and you feel good, calm energy flow through you.

On the other hand, we also have warning signs—they are like grey clouds quietly gathering before the storm is unleashed.

Signs of "Woah, Better Step Back Here"

- When your throat feels tighter. Or when you're hunched or crouched, as if you're trying to protect yourself.

- When there's a nauseous or heavy feeling in your chest and stomach, or a bitter, acidic taste in your mouth.

- When your skin crawls and you're on edge.

- When the hair on the back of your neck stands. (This is usually a huge sign that something isn't right.)

- When your heart starts beating very fast and you feel like you're falling into panic mode.

- You feel like there's a cloud of pressure on your shoulders or around your neck.

- When it feels like time passes really slowly.

- When you feel the anxious need to drink alcohol.

The Time When Signs Washed All Over Me

I felt very clear signs when I went house-hunting early this year. My bank application got pre-approved within 24 hours, and the bank officer recommended a real estate broker. Soon, I had three viewings lined up—smooth like a breeze!

The first apartment was in a neighborhood I liked, too bad it wasn't available anymore when I got there. My intuition told me it wasn't actually a big loss because while at the lobby, I felt the environment was a little cold and unfriendly. So I went with my gut and trusted that I would find something better. Soon.

The second condo was an immediate turn-off—I didn't like it the moment I walked in. My body didn't open up to it either. It was definitely the wrong place for me.

The third one was different. It was in a great location and set at an excellent price. There was a sense of community in that neighbourhood, and the building itself felt friendly. On the outside, it felt promising. When I walked into the lobby towards the front desk, my shoulders relaxed and my gut felt comfortable. The couches, the tables, the way the natural light shone in—they fell into place perfectly. They felt right.

"Hi, I'm here for a viewing", I said to the receptionist. Heck, even *that* made me thrilled!

Once my broker opened the door, I stepped in and felt as if the apartment was warmly welcoming me. My adrenalin shot up. Excitement pumped through my body and I felt like jumping up and down. Like a kid, I clapped with joy.

There was not a trace of hesitation or doubt in me—I was ready and wanted to close the deal as soon as possible. These "right" feelings and my body's reactions all combined to tell me that this was the right place for me to call home.

When I was going through depression, I had difficulty trusting men in my relationships. I knew it was because of my father. But when I was in that hole, I wasn't able to help myself make the right call.

I kept picking the wrong men—men who were not emotionally available; men who were not career-focused; men with Peter Pan Syndrome (i.e. people who refuse to grow up and take responsibility for what's going on in their lives); men who didn't understand that relationships could only work through trust and communication; men who still looked at other women and strayed.

I needed a deeper connection, but they were not willing to give it. My intuition told me to let go of these unreliable guys, but I was too afraid. I feared letting go. So I chose not to trust my gut, I chose to deny it.

The Time It Hit Me Worst

There was this particular guy, X. He and I had been friends with benefits for years. We knew we wouldn't end up in marriage, but we still continued to see each other.

Until one day, he stopped.

What happened was like a hurricane blowing over me. I couldn't stop calling him. And when he didn't return my calls, my mind kept churning, *Why is he doing this? Why won't he pick up my calls?*

On and on it went. I kept calling and kept asking myself these questions. And I just couldn't sleep. I stayed in bed miserable. When I went to work, I wasn't able to function. Sometimes, I chose not to go at all. At that point I realized that things were severely wrong and I had to do something about it!

In the past, friends and family would advise me to seek professional help, but I always took it with a grain of salt. This time, when my gut prompted me to, I finally listened. That inner voice created a real sense of urgency—I'd got to get help!

I FINALLY took that first step.

You know how most people make a mental list of criteria for the therapist/doctor/dentist/lawyer/date they want? "They have got to be a certain age frame. They must have at least ten years of experience. They must have hundreds of reviews!" On and on that list would go.

I switched on my laptop and tried to calm my racing heart.

On a national website that listed psychologists, I typed in my zip code. Scroll, scroll, scroll. One profile picture after another flew upwards my screen.

Hmm, this therapist looks stern and very professional but doesn't feel like someone I'd be comfortable with. That one looks energetic and cheery but … nah, not what I'm looking for.

Until I came across the picture of a therapist in her 70s. She wasn't grinning widely. Her smile was warm and comforting. An aura of patience beamed from her face. My intuition told me she was someone I would be "safe" with.

Click. I booked an appointment straightaway.

When I met her for the first time, I knew she was the one (yes, sounds like Therapy-Tinder). She was personable and she even had a therapy dog - a King Charles Cavalier. Everything about her pointed to an encouraging direction. I talked to her about my father, and those men who had made me feel very small about myself. During that first session alone, a small weight lifted from my heart.

I saw her twice a month for the next eight years. My therapist got me through that worse-than-hell period and it took an awfully long time, but I eventually worked my way out of it. Now that I look back on that frustrating period, I feel so relieved! I feel a lot stronger and steadier. I'm no longer afraid.

CHAPTER FIVE

WHERE DOES OUR INTUITION LIE?

Where does our intuition lie? Is it in our gut? Or in our brain? Where, exactly, in our brain?

Right vs. Left

As it turns out, our intuition lies in our right brain, which is responsible for:

- Recognizing faces

- Identifying emotions

- Showing emotions

- Colors

- Music & Rhythm

- Imagination/Daydreaming

- Arts/Creativity

- Intuition

On the other hand, our left brain is strong in:

- Analytical thinking

- Logic

- Math

- Language

- Sequence

Women have a deeper connection to our intuition. This is because we have more nerve fibres called corpus callosum. The reason you hear that women are more intuitive is because we have more nerve fibres connecting the right brain and the left brain, which makes us more inclined to listen to both sides.

Our right brain develops quicker than our left—a few weeks after we are born, we start to recognize the faces of our family, their vocal and facial expressions.

The truth is, we start to train and use our intuitive power a lot sooner than we may realize. Ever since we were kids, we've been learning how to read expressions from the adults. Every minute of every day, our brains are picking up clues from our environment to help us get through every situation and interaction.

For example, if we say something as a joke and our friend turns up her nose, we sense disapproval. Or at the very least, disagreement.

When a colleague folds his arms and leans back during a meeting, we sense disengagement.

When someone speaks with rising intonation, we feel a question is being asked (and hence, we sense uncertainty or her desire for you to agree with what she's saying).

Or how about before we enter a risky situation, and we feel something bad is about to happen? Like a premonition?

Unfortunately, regardless of all these signs, we often dismiss our "senses" (a right-brain activity) because we want to remain rational (a left-brain activity).

Picking up Signals & Interpreting Them

Have you ever sat in front of a salesperson, listening to her talk, knowing that what she's saying makes sense, and yet somehow you felt uncomfortable with it? The time when what someone says sounds right, but you feel something is off?

Those feelings come from our intuition. Our right brain is like a radar, it can pick up even the subtlest of signals. But if we don't figure out a way to interpret those signals, chances are we'll just brush them aside.

And this is where our left brain comes in: through reasoning, it can help us interpret our signals.

The key is to stay open—welcome what your senses are telling you, however subtle they may be. Then try to interpret what they mean through an open heart of experience and knowledge.

Are You Fixing Your Problems Right?

Let's say there's an issue right now and our gut sends out signals of anxiety. That message of *"Something weird is going on"* reaches our brain, and we need to figure it out.

Do we work it out through our left or right brain?

If you recall, our left brain is straightforward and based on reasoning. It goes by a linear process. It thinks step-by-step.

Our right brain, however, is not logical. It's connected to our creativity and feelings. Its thinking process is random and non-linear.

So many of us try to solve our emotional (i.e. non-linear) problems through reasoning or analysis (linear solutions). We keep churning and tossing and turning. And we feel stuck! (That's right, the hamster running on the wheel again till its poor heart gives out). Then we blame ourselves for being stupid.

We question why we can't seem to get over something, and we feel powerless and stuck. But we never once realize that we've been attempting to work out our non-linear problems through the wrong method.

This isn't about being smart or stupid. It may not even be about being strong or weak. Our left brain is just not able to solve our right-brain problems!

Remember this: On some level, our left brain *can* help us with some part of our problem—but it cannot untangle a complicated emotional issue all on its own. It needs our right brain to do that. Through intuition.

CHAPTER SIX

OUR INTUITION AT SCHOOL & WORK

If our intuition can be such a powerful tool in our lives, why don't we use it more often? Are we so out of touch with our intuition that we cannot hear it? Is it that we simply cannot interpret what our bodies want to tell us? Or is it because using our intuition doesn't sound as "solid" as using rationality or logic? That it might make us appear ditzy?

Our Education System Doesn't Sharpen This Skill

Yes, Mathematics is important. So is scientific research and art history and geography—getting our facts right is, and will always be critical. The ability to reason well improves your rank on the hot debate team. Even when you're in a creative writing class, you need to analyse everything—the poem contents, the author's intentions, the writing techniques used, etc. And if you're on a sports team, you need to learn different game strategies. There seems to be a system for everything.

Analytical skills and factual knowledge are invaluable—we need to keep learning and constantly develop our practical life skills to keep up with the world. But what about honing our other skills of understanding the world?

Sure, we may have talks about paying attention to our feelings and classes on Creativity. But those stuff they taught us in school are rarely scheduled for daily pursuit or constant learning and understanding and growing. That is, we haven't been taught to tap into our intuition daily.

Let's take Art classes for example. When we were in kindergarten, we were always encouraged to "draw what you want," and "express yourself however you like!" But what happened to that creative freedom later on? Grades happened. We were graded for our artistic techniques and skills. How on earth do people grade self-expression? I have no idea! Ultimately, we had to please the person grading our creativity. Our intuitive sense to create became restricted. (Then further on, we were given the impression that Art is not as important as Arithmetic...)

Throughout our formative years, we were rarely encouraged to trust our gut or to develop intuitive solutions to our problems daily. We were never even taught how to get in touch with our inner selves!

Bringing Intuition into Our Workplace

Granted, we have great and not-so-great news here.

The good news is, there has been a blooming interest in intuition over recent years—just look at the self-help sections at your library or local bookstore. Are there now more books on this subject? How about the reviews of books on Intuition on Amazon and Goodreads? Are there more people reading on and talking about Intuition? The truth is, many people are interested—and not just young working adults, but also corporate bigwigs.

In a 2015 Forbes article, executive coach/author/ speaker Bonnie Marcus called our intuition *"the greatest resource for making sound decisions"*.

Big companies have started to call for focus groups to get feedback on the presentation of their brand— they ask participants questions like the preferred color of the buttons, the position of those buttons, or the type of font they like, etc. And when they do, they don't expect people to analyse at all, they just want to know their intuitive impressions of how the website "feels" to them. And there are never right or wrong answers!

In other professions, intuition is used to meet emotional needs or to solve a specific "work" problem. Take the healthcare industry, for example. Nurses spend most of their time caring and tending to their patients' needs. While they seem to perform their everyday tasks routinely, they understand and constantly use their intuitive wisdom—often allowing it to override clinical evaluations or decisions to prevent a disaster or emergency. Consider remarks like this:

"Something about this patient seems off today even though the readings are normal. I'd better get a doctor here."

The more experienced a nurse is, the more they can rely on and trust their intuition.

Another example comes from the creative field. Writers and artists often tap into their gut feelings when they are deep at work. Write about this character more?

Delete that scene? To choreograph my dance this way or that?

When they get stuck, writers sometimes jot down their thoughts in a journal or ask questions. Then they wait for their brain to gradually sort things out—and the answers often quietly announce themselves during a long walk or a hot shower, or simply after a good night's sleep!

These days, more and more people are interested in learning about and using their intuition. If only more were actually *that* comfortable admitting to it!

The not-so-great news is that those who *are* comfortable admitting to using our intuition, like me, have difficulty defending our intuitive decisions. I work in Silicon Valley and test websites for a living. My official job position is Quality Assurance Manager. You can imagine all the data, analyses, and reports surrounding me everyday, right? So how does someone so fascinated with Intuition and making decisions based on her gut fit in a place like this?

To be honest, sometimes it's excruciating. Once, at a meeting with my manager, I gave him feedback on a website and he wasn't taking it well at all.

"The search bar needs to be longer", I said finally.

"Why does it need to be longer?" he asked.

"My intuition says so."

His eyes narrowed. *"Why did your intuition say that?"*

I didn't know what to say—I knew I had that information, but I didn't know how to explain or verbalise my gut-brain connection backed up by five years of experience testing websites!

It was difficult for me to explain my decision because I didn't trust my intuition to be a legitimate resource back then—there wasn't a way for me to tick the boxes on my intuitive judgement. If only I knew how to develop my intuition to be *so strong* that I wouldn't doubt it and, in turn, influence others not to question it.

Now that you know more about your intuition, you won't have to spend so much time ruminating about your past and worrying about your future. You would have this ironclad inner security that can withstand any outside force (be it an asshole at work, a judgmental client, the loss of your job, a divorce, or sickness).

CHAPTER SEVEN

HOW TO SNUGGLE UP TO YOUR INTUITION

Here are some incredibly easy, yet effective methods that have helped me over the years. Pick one and go with it. See how it turns out. And when you're ready, try the next one!

1. Jot down your dreams

Keep a dream journal or notebook close by. When you get up in the morning, before you get hustled away, take a few minutes to write down what you dreamed the night before. Jot them down, even if they are ugly, broken sentences. Point form, key words and phrases, whichever works for you. Don't worry about writing perfect sentences or thoughts!

Then go online and do a quick search on what they may mean. What does jumping off a cliff mean? What does taking flight or drowning mean? Who could that snake represent in my reality? Or how about when babies start showing up in your dreams? Check out the interpretations and pick the one you feel most "in tune" with.

Years ago, my therapist introduced me to this technique of writing down my dreams and then interpreting them the way I wanted to.

Wait. The way you wanted to? You mean there's no right or wrong interpretation?

Yep. Exactly. Our dreams rarely make sense. They are not rational. They are, like many things in life, not black or white. So don't get fixated on all the meanings. If a particular interpretation resonates with you, that's your intuition telling you to explore more in that area.

I always find this stage interesting: That of all the things I can take away from my dream, I choose this specific meaning. Why is that so? What does this person or thing in my dream mean to me and only me?

Using our conscious mind to understand what our subconscious mind is telling us is fascinating—it makes me eager to dream so I can understand myself and connect with my inner self better!

Another interesting thing that can happen through dream journaling is the heart-stopping experience of Deja Vu. Like meeting someone for the first time yet feeling as though you've known each other for years. Or when you go to a place you've never been before but strangely, you feel like you have!

Back in 2011, I was on my first trip abroad. My train in Paris had arrived and I boarded it to make my way to Berlin. Soon, the train zoomed off softly.

"In Love with Dusk" by Keep Shelly in Athens played through my earphones. The beats moved me in the same tunnel of excitement the train transported me to another European adventure. And for a minute, my heart stopped.

Goosebumps on my back.

I looked around and the strangest case of deja vu fell upon me. *Woah, I've been on this train before, listening to this very song.*

That exact moment had happened before. But it was my first trip overseas! How crazy was that?

The reason we encounter this familiar sensation during a specific situation is because we have been there in our dreams. Through dream journaling, we can uncover these weirdly wonderful re-visits. I had this insight during a therapy session and it blew my mind.

2. Awaken your intuition with tarot cards

Buy a pack and start playing. In fact, play every day—it's easy, and it's fun. Pick three cards: one in the morning, one in the afternoon, and one in the evening. Breathe and focus when you pick your cards. Then, as with your dream interpretations, go online and do a search on what your cards may mean and try to connect them with what's going on in your life.

I often look for meanings from my cards. What does the Queen of Wands mean in my life right now? *Am I on fire with what I'm doing?*

How about the Two of Cups? It signifies relationships and affection. *Am I lacking affection? Is there a particular relationship I want to nurture right now? Or am I in need of some self-love? How does this card play into my life at this moment?*

Or what about the King of Swords appearing? *Does he symbolise an authoritative figure—maybe my boss? Could this be me feeling intimidated to ask my boss for a raise or something similar?*

Our intuition works through symbolism. Card readings can provide us with insights on how we feel on a deeper level about the situations we're facing. They can also guide us through sorting out our emotions and coming up with decisions we feel the most comfortable with.

Like the King of Swords example again—the king is a logical person who thinks in a rational way. Drawing this card might symbolize that I would need to approach my boss in this rational way, too, instead of trying to meet him on an emotional level.

Again, what we learn from the meanings and the interpretations we pick is up to us. This is how our intuition reminds us that *"Hey, this issue is bothering me."* This is how our intuition steers us towards understanding ourselves better.

And the best part is that there are absolutely no right or wrong answers—you get to choose what to believe and accept as your guidance. Cool, huh?

3. Keep a brainstorm journal.

Okay, I have a confession to make, and it is going to sound ironic: I hate writing about things that happen to me on a daily basis. I cannot go ten pages into *"Oh my God, this stupid thing happened to me today. I blah, blah, blah …"* I wouldn't know what the goal is!

However, if I set an intention on what I want to achieve, I'm happy to write it all down so I can explore it further. For example, if you have been wondering about stuff like:

"What am I passionate about?"

"What should I pursue as my career?"

"What do I most want to do?"

You might want to brainstorm and keep asking yourself those questions. Then write down all your answers. Make a list. Go as long as you want. No judgment involved!

You'll be in awe of all the answers you collect. Some of them you'd never expect. And that'll be your intuition giving you a nudge towards what you should explore more of.

See this as a way of you speaking to yourself, asking lots and lots of questions—or even the same question multiple times, until you're ready to move forward. Give your brain some time to digest. Your intuition might just pop up with an answer when you least expect it to.

4. Write, write, write

- Write about the times you *trusted* your intuition and *got* what you wanted. The next time you feel unsure whether you should trust your gut feelings, this note will serve as a reminder that you DO have inner wisdom guiding you.

- Write about the times you *didn't* trust your intuition and *didn't get* what you wanted. The next time you doubt your gut feelings again, it will remind you of all those painful times you didn't heed your own intuition— *"See, I KNEW that would happen. I should've listened to myself!"*

- Write about the times you *trusted* your intuition but *didn't get* what you wanted. The truth is, our intuition guides us towards actions that we believe in, but it doesn't guarantee anything. There's no guarantee that things will always work out well. The only success it guarantees is honing your ability to trust yourself and make the best decision you feel to be right.

Getting closer to our intuition takes practice. It takes real action. Which method would you like to try? Go for it!

CHAPTER EIGHT

USE YOUR INTUITION TO UNPACK YOUR EMOTIONAL BAGGAGE

Remember right at the beginning of this book, I talked about my search for happiness and how my research kept bringing me back to meditation? It was through meditation that I got in touch with my intuition and that was when I unpacked my emotional baggage.

I'll be the first to admit that I have emotional baggage. Big, fat, ugly ones. And so do you. Most often, we are willing to acknowledge our emotional overload only when we face something terrible, like the loss of a loved one, a broken heart that won't mend, a nasty divorce, a huge financial hit, a painful miscarriage, and everything else that leaves a scar. Unless we take the time to unpack, those burdens will never become lighter.

No matter how you brush them aside, they will only get heavier.

In this chapter, I'm going to dive deep into a few different ways to meditate so that you can unpack your emotional baggage, too.

Meditation

Meditation is powerful in sharpening your intuition because your mind will be quiet.

Bear in mind that like with any new skill, you will find it challenging to get the hang of meditation at first. It's easy to get distracted. Your mind will wander for miles and your thoughts will shriek and dart around or zoom off on wild tangents. Relax though, this is all normal! Even advanced meditators have gone through this monkey phase.

The good news is you don't need to struggle to achieve a peaceful state of mind. Beneath your chatter, that quiet, calm, confident mind already exists. And meditation is a way of allowing that state of you to emerge.

No need for new gears, nothing. Just you and a quiet spot. Sweet, right?

3 Favorite Meditation Methods

They are: binaural beats meditation, mindfulness meditation, and mantra meditation. You don't have to study all three of them. If you have trouble taming your mind, I suggest you skip right ahead to mantra meditation. Simple guidance through any of these techniques will help you establish a good meditative routine. Let's begin.

Binaural Beats Meditation

Did you know that meditation allows us to change our brain frequency? Our brains are made up of about 20 billion neurons that generate electro-chemical vibrational impulses. These electrical impulses are how our brain cells communicate with one another and they form patterns, which we call brain waves or frequencies.

Essentially, we have five main brain wave patterns:

1. Gamma — The Gamma state is the best time to learn and retain information. It's when we are at our most focused state.

2. Beta — We spend most of our day in the Beta state. It is the alert state of mind we are in when we perform our daily functions like working or thinking.

3. Alpha — The Alpha state is when we are relaxed and calm. We are brought to a more lucid or reflective awareness.

4. Theta — This is where we begin to go into a meditative state. We are more intuitive and can visualize what we want better.

5. Delta — The Delta state is the state of being in a deep, dreamless sleep.

When you listen to sounds of a specific frequency, your brain waves begin to synchronize with that frequency. You can use sound meditation to induce a desired mental state by manipulating your brain waves.

How to Practice Binaural Beats Meditation

So many people give up on meditation because they find it frustratingly impossible to focus and get desired results. This technique is really helpful for beginners. It acts as a shortcut toward getting the best from your brain waves.

To begin, search for free online downloads or examples of binaural beats meditation. Then sit and listen. Surrender to the audio tone and allow the binaural beats to synchronize your brain waves. You'll enter one of the meditative states (usually alpha or theta) rapidly.

Seriously, you don't have to think about anything at all. Just listen and let your brain waves respond. Best practiced with headphones on, this is a natural and effective way to bring your mind calmness every day.

Mindfulness Meditation

Want an easy way to integrate meditation into your daily routine? Just pay attention.

Pay attention to what? To the present moment! Basic mindfulness is the practice of paying attention to the present without any judgment. You accept what goes through your head. It's the ability to become aware of your physical sensations in the present moment and "see" your thoughts and emotions more clearly. (And when your thoughts become way too negative, you get to keep them in check.)

How to Practice Mindfulness Meditation

Remind yourself throughout the day to be aware. Be aware of this very moment and feel it. Stop to breathe deeply, recall what you're doing and why you're doing it, and take stock of how you're feeling.

Practice mindfulness when you're washing the dishes, or taking a shower, or driving your car, or before sending out an email. Notice how you feel when you're doing these routine tasks. Acknowledging how you feel can ease the clutter in your mind that's causing your energy level to spike or dip.

If you're often stressed out about life, stop to appreciate what is happening *around* and *within* you, even for a few seconds. It is an incredibly effective way of bringing your mind back to a state of calm. Practice it again and again. Eventually, mindful meditation will be integrated seamlessly into everything you do. And that's when you can better hear your intuition giving you insights on unpacking whatever's stressing you out.

Mantra Meditation

The word "Mantra" comes from India and is said to mean "a mental device" or "an instrument of the mind." Reciting a mantra or repeating a word or phrase gives your mind something to focus on. Perfect for those of us with monkey minds!

Common ancient mantras are "Om" (the sacred sound of Hinduism) and "Om Mane Padme Hum" (of Buddhism). An interesting note is that mantras also hold ancient spiritual meaning which can transform you through meditation. But you don't have to know anything about this to experience the benefits of mantra meditation. Simply repeating a phrase that calms and helps you focus is good enough.

How to Practice Mantra Meditation

The beauty of a mantra like "om" is in its simplicity. It is the most basic and powerful of all mantras, and it is easy to repeat. Its sound is said to symbolically tune us into the sound of the universe, connecting us with all living things.

On the other hand, if you're feeling creative, come up with your own mantra. What word or phrase resonates with you the most? Keep it simple so that it is easy to repeat.

Chant the mantra out loud at the beginning of your meditation then continue internally. Or if you prefer speaking it all the way throughout your session, go for it. Either way, the benefits will begin to show themselves with time and acceptance.

Meditation is about showing up for yourself again and again. It is about the acceptance of both good and bad days. It is about connecting with your truest, highest self. It is NOT about being perfect. Most of all, it is about allowing your individual journey to be adaptable, illuminating, and pleasurable. So let your practice develop naturally and enjoy it!

Use Your Brains to Unpack

Once you learn to get to that calm inner self through meditation, you can tap into your right-brain (where your intuition rests) to help you unpack your heavy emotional load.

Or you can use your left brain to help you unpack, too. Through this ABC method:

A stands for the Activating Event, or the trigger that provokes an emotional response from you.

B is the Belief that decides what your emotional response is going to be.

C is the Coping Mechanism or the reaction, either offensive or defensive, that you think is suitable for that situation.

My Emotional Baggage Is the Fear of Abandonment

Deep down, I know my friends would never abandon me. But when they don't return my calls, I would be triggered into a panic mode (yup, that's my Activating Trigger - unreturned phone calls).

The Belief I would hold in my mind would be: I'm not important. Because my father did not reply to my texts and calls, I transferred this fear of abandonment or insecurity toward my friends. My father's abandonment happened in the past and I carried this to my present, affecting all my current relationships.

My Coping Mechanism back then? Ha, I would keep calling them non-stop. Or if they called me back eventually, I'd start screaming at them like a toddler. (I'll admit, not my finest moments.)

My Coping Mechanism now is to breathe in deeply for one minute. With more self-awareness, I'm more empowered and in control of my emotions. I won't freak out so easily and when I do over-react, I can be honest and apologize to my friends.

So whichever way you choose to unpack, try to get to that quiet, calm state and see what weighs you down. The first few things that pop up are usually clues.

This is an emotional process. Don't worry or be afraid of being "triggered." Any emotions you feel throughout, be it procrastination, anxiety, or doubts, are okay. It's not a bad thing to feel them. (On the contrary, if you don't feel anything at all, you might need to do this a few times before your issues are willing to surface.)

Your intuition is so powerful you can unpack and heal through it. One step at a time.

YOUR TOP THREE QUESTIONS ABOUT INTUITION

B y now, you *should* have some questions about how your intuition works. That's perfectly normal. We cannot begin to understand something we don't question, right?

So here goes the top three questions people tend to have regarding their intuition, as well as my personal interpretations:

Question 1: Is Our Intuition Always Right?

Our intuition doesn't always give a trustworthy answer because our emotional conditions, or mental states, aren't always calm enough to draw clear conclusions either. When we are in a bad mood, or a "dark place," we are most likely stressed out. There's tension in our body and our heart feels squeezed. Our thoughts are congested and we can't hear them clearly. We interpret situations in black and white instead of considering other possibilities.

For example, if we're already tensed up and a colleague snaps at us, we may jump to the conclusion that she secretly hates us, or that she's a total bitch—without ever considering the possibility that she, otherwise a nice person, is also just having an off-day.

When our mood dips into negativity, we tend lose focus and may become desperate to find something to hold on to. In that restless state, we don't feel like taking chances—we want to find the right answer, the right solution, right now! We are driven by fear, anxiety, or frustration, and that's never a good way to tap into our intuition.

When you are frustrated and yearning for quick answers, you have certain expectations you hope to meet. And you secretly beg your intuition to give you those right answers. You're trying to *force* it to answer.

"Does he love me?"

Your ego wants your intuition to say yes. But that's not what our intuition is here for. It isn't here to serve our egos.

If you want to know FOR SURE if your intuition is right, first you need to make sure your emotional condition is calm—make sure you stay open to whatever answer that comes.

And then it'll come. Even if it's not the answer you are expecting, and even if it's not the answer you want, it will be the answer you need.

Question 2: How Do I Know That's My Intuition or My Desire Talking?

Our desires are usually based on instant gratification. Like if we buy that pair of shoes, we'd be happy. And yes, we are. We are very happy for that afternoon. After that, we sort of regret splurging. That's impulse—the energy there is urgent and pushy. It satisfies you almost immediately but you can also feel it slipping away after a while.

Our intuition is a lot calmer. Its energy draws us deeper. For example, when you go on a romantic date with a man you are very attracted to. And the question about whether or not to have sex that night seems to be pushing at you. "Should I sleep with him tonight? Will he think I'm too eager? Or is that what he wants, too? What if he blows me off after sex?"

Yada, yada, yada. Both desire and anxiety grabbing the mic.

But if you feel that this person might be *the right one* to go on a long-term relationship with, and a thought like that gives you a calm sense of happiness (like sunshine spreading over the fields in a Lifetime movie), then that is your intuition talking.

Learn to feel the difference through your body.

Question 3: How Do I Know That's My Intuition or My Instinct Talking?

Instinct fears the new, intuition embraces it

Instincts are what has kept the human civilization alive for centuries. We cannot even grasp the world our ancestors had to live in.

Ultimately, it's your natural instinct is to appreciate what's familiar and what's safe – not what's out there, outside the comfort zone.

However… here comes the BIG BUT.

There aren't as many threats in the modern world. You don't have to run and hide from a grizzly bear every other day. You don't have to walk miles to find clean water to drink.

And in a world like ours, well… relying *too much* on your instincts may keep you stuck in place. Your strongest instincts translate into your biggest fears.

What good comes out of fears anyway?

See my point here?

Contrary to that, intuition is like a light guiding you towards something new – but nonetheless, equally good, if not better – for you. A shining star on the horizon you follow to arrive where you're meant to be.

I like to think that intuition is how the human civilization has advanced. Someone listened to what their intuition has to say and started to explore the new.

Can you imagine if they didn't?

CHAPTER TEN

TO INTUITION & BEYOND

We're almost reaching the end of this book. So far, we've talked about the science behind intuition, and the use of intuition at work and in our social life. I've shared techniques on how you can become more in touch with your inner voice. And I've answered the top questions you might have regarding your intuition.

So, what's next? Something beyond, for sure! Beyond the boundaries of everyday practicalities—and *into* our spiritual awakening.

Our Fourth State

We often hear about our conscious, subconscious, and unconscious states. But did you know there is actually a fourth? It's our superconscious mind—in spirituality terms, it's a state of heightened awareness.

Awareness of what, you may ask? Of everything, of how our world works, of knowledge of the universe through the ages. It's true wisdom that eradicates our ego and enhances our intuition.

"Intuition has nothing to do with reflection – it comes directly from a level of cosmic wisdom. Everything that is being learned already exists in an energy form in the cosmos; each thought and all inventions already exist."

— Swami Durgananda, PhD.
Meditation, Subconscious Mind and Intuition

My Own Spiritual Process

I am guided by cosmic intelligence. It took me a while to realise that everything that has happened in my life has happened in such a way to get me onto this path. They have happened *for* me. I feel blessed to have awakened that deeply spiritual part inside me. To be "chosen" to connect with the vast universe out there.

Of the unknown, of the mysterious.

Of many miraculous transformations.

At this point in writing, my spiritual awakening process has just started. I've come to learn about the greys of life—nothing is ever purely black or white. Nothing is only what we see and know. There are things beyond. Things that didn't make sense to me previously but kept happening.

And my intuitive practice has helped me figure out just what they mean for me. That my journey, the life purpose that I used to keep searching for but couldn't find till now, is to keep interacting with others who want to expand their spirituality. That I am meant to be someone else's guide now.

I'd love to teach my unique way of achieving inner peace through understanding your mind, body, and spirit. I'd like to help you stand firmer on your feet through inner self-development. I'd also like to remove the stigma or reservations some people have of Intuition and Spirituality. My intuitive abilities have helped me develop clairvoyance (the power of clear-seeing) and clairaudience (the power of clear-hearing) and Life has been so much more interesting. No, it is not "woo woo" stuff—it is much more than that. And it is more relatable to you than you think!

There is a bright, new world outside our transactional, material life. And I want to be your guide towards it.

CHAPTER ELEVEN

FULL CIRCLE

I don't believe in coincidences—nothing is that random. Things happen for a reason. Mostly good reasons. You came across my website or social media page not by some flimsy, woozy chance. I believe you chose to download this book because your intuition gave you a nudge.

My intuition has given me many nudges, including exposures to tarot card reading sessions and spirit guides (spirits of loved ones who have passed on) through a medium. It has led me into meditating. It has led me into astral travelling, an area I intend to explore deeper. It has also guided me towards starting my spirituality brand and sharing what I've learned with you. This book you're reading right now is a fruit of it.

Bernadette Balla: Your Guide to Spirituality

In July 2016, I took the first step in establishing my brand by building my website. My Instagram and Facebook platforms soon grew as well. I made sure to reach out to others who were feeling lost like I once was. I wanted them to know someone was there for them.

I soon started to receive messages from several young women who told me their stories and after guiding them towards self-healing, they felt understood and much less alone. That warmed my heart and fuelled my determination in seeing my work cast more light in more lives!

Fears, Uncertainties, Plus Something Else

Now that I have guidance from my intuition and spirituality, everything is going to be a walk in the park, right?

Nope.

There is always something to tackle as we reach different stages of growth and awakening. For me, writing this book has been liberating but now that it's out, it's also quite scary. Because while other entrepreneurs fear failure, I fear success.

This is perhaps the greatest lesson of all, the most insightful lesson led by my intuitive journey: We don't get to choose what happens to us, but we get to choose how to deal with them.

I didn't have a choice when my father walked out on us. But I've now chosen his abandonment to be the reason behind my practice—to overcome this sense of emptiness. To get me to an emotionally fulfilling place by being here for myself always. To bring me to an unshakeable level of belief that my life is so much more than I can imagine. And to nudge me into opening my heart so I can receive more wisdom. Wisdom that I may share with you to bring you comfort or inspiration.

Here's one more piece of it as my way to thank you for reading this book: I'm sharing my personal affirmation, a very simple statement that I say three times, the last being the loudest and clearest.

My life is growing better every day.

My life is growing *better* every day.

My life is growing better *every day*.

Did You Enjoy Learning More About Your Intuition?

If this book has helped you connect with your superpower in any way, please leave a review here! Then share the love and tell your friends, for everyone needs this journey of deeper self-love. And it all starts from within ourselves.

BONUS CHAPTER

Welcome to my intuition quiz!

I've created this quiz for you to help you explore your intuition further. It'll also help you determine how strong your intuition is.

Simply **circle each answer** that's true for yourself. And when you've finished, **add the score together** and **read the results in the end!**

1. You are a good judge of character.

a) No, actually, I have a knack for picking horrible people as my friends!

b) Rarely, though I can tell if something is *reaaaaaally* off

c) Sometimes I am, sometimes I'm not, depends on the person

d) Most of the time I am—I've had a couple of slips but nothing that would worry me

e) I can always judge someone just by giving them a glance. I don't even need to spend a lot of time near them to find out who they really are.

2. You simply know whether someone is honest or lying to you.

    a)   Nope, I just hope people don't lie to me and that's it (but they still do)

    b)   Rarely, I still struggle with this

    c)   Sometimes I do, sometimes I don't

    d)   I can usually sense if something's fishy in a story

    e)   I always know if someone's being dishonest with me—I can simply tell right away!

3. Animals and kids like you. You are always approached by animals and kids in the park.

    a)   The kids I've babysat didn't cry, does that count?

    b)   Not really, though my nieces and nephews love me!

    c)   It depends on the day I'm having, though most kids like me!

    d)   Yes, I'm fairly sure this is true for me

    e)   This always happens to me! Kids are smiling at me and dogs wave their tails when they see me!

4. You are creative. You can easily explore different parts of your creativity and express them in different ways (writing, painting, singing, etc.)

a) Not in a million years—I just lack all creativity

b) I've written a winning essay in college once and wear colorful clothes daily, but that's about it

c) I'm very creative but don't use my creativity as much as I'd like to

d) OMG, yes! This is one of my favorite ways to relax, a day can't go by without me painting/writing/singing

e) I've always been very creative. I also use my creativity to earn most—if not all—of my income.

5. Your intuition helps you stay away from danger (or it has helped save your life in the past).

a) Nah, I don't think that will ever happen

b) Not as often as I'd like to see this happening though I still stay away from dark alleys

c) Well, it hasn't exactly saved my life but my intuition helped me stay away from danger a few times

d) Yeah, I've made more than a few right moves relying on my gut alone

e) I've avoided a major accident in the past and survived just by listening to my gut.

6. You get guidance from a bigger force whenever feeling lost and confused.

a) No, never—where do I find this thing?

b) This has only happened once or twice when I was really in trouble

c) Sometimes this happens but I really have to be feeling desperate. Other times, I just deal with the facts in front of me.

d) Most of the time I'm able to find an answer to my troubles if I listen closely

e) Of course, how else do you make decisions in life?

7. You are good at reading even the slightest body signs. You can tell if something's off instantly.

a) Sadly, I'm not. I have no idea how people read body language

b) If someone's giving off really bad vibes then maybe I'll notice

c) Depends on the other person really, maybe if their vibes are strong enough

d) Almost always though some people are hard to crack!

e) Yeah, and the weirdest part is that I don't really try to do this—it just comes naturally!

8. Whenever talking to someone, you know how the person talking to you feels.

a) I don't, and I've embarrassed myself in the past by not noticing

b) I can tell sometimes if someone's having a bad day

c) If they're really sad or really happy, I'd notice

d) Pretty often I do, though some people are really good at hiding emotions!

e) Almost instantly, even if they're trying to hide their true feelings.

9. You experience pain & discomfort if a loved one is experiencing them as well. You know when someone is ill/having trouble or maybe even dying.

a) Never, can people really do this?

b) I wasn't happy that a loved one was sick, but only felt emotional discomfort (couldn't tell anything on my own)

c) Sometimes I feel emotionally drained without knowing the reason behind it, and later find out a loved one was going through something at the same exact time

d) This has happened a few times and I always call to check if everyone is all right. If I experience cramps in my stomach/chest/heart area, then something's really wrong

e) Yes, this often happens to me, including the physical sensations and the pain! I can sense what my loved ones are up to even if miles away!

10. Empathy is one of your strongest suits. You catch other people's feelings even if you don't want to.

a)   Nope, how do you sense other people's feelings?

b)   Not really, but I'm trying to learn how to become more emphatic

c)   I'm empathic enough to know something's wrong and offer support when needed

d)   Often, especially if we're talking about the vibes of people close to me

e)   Always, and I end up needing to spend time on my own to shake off the vibes from everyone around me that I unintentionally pick up.

11. Each time you meet someone new, you get positive/negative vibes about them that turn out to be true once you get to know them better.

a) This has never happened to me

b) It's happened only once when I met that weird girl from college and got some strong negative vibes from her

c) I'd say this happens sometimes, but nothing out of the ordinary

d) Not only do I often pick up someone's vibe right from the start, most of the time I turn out to be right

e) I do! I can fully rely on what my gut is telling me about someone because it's always right!

12. Your body is giving you physical signs about a person whenever you spend time with someone.

a) Never, what are the signs I need to look out for?

b) I got a chill down my neck once when that creepy guy next door walked past me in the hallway

c) Sometimes, though they're not strong signs. I just feel more relaxed around some people

d) Quite often, especially if that person's energy is negative, I immediately get anxious!

e) This happens every single time I meet someone new. I know it right away if I can trust them or not.

13. You feel confident enough about the direction or path you've chosen to follow.

a) What direction?

b) I just did what everyone else around me was doing, haven't looked deeper at stuff

c) Not every single day, but then something big happens and I know it's a sign that I'm on the right path!

d) Most days though I also have my doubts—I guess that's normal too

e) I get daily signs and reminders that I'm walking in the right direction.

14. You listen to your gut when making a major decision.

a) Nah, only cold facts and logic for me, please!

b) Rarely, perhaps I'd do this in a life or death situation

c) Sometimes I do, sometimes I don't, it depends on how much I can hear my gut talking. I also like to look at the facts in front of me!

d) I definitely take my gut feeling into consideration on all of my major life decisions

e) Yup, and I don't even need to look at the facts. I know that my intuition is telling me what's the right move to make.

15. You've followed your gut ever since a young age. You were "different" than the rest.

a) Never, no idea what you're talking about here

b) I don't remember I was different than the rest, but I remember I tried to be kind

c) Only if something was very obvious

d) I was often able to tell right from wrong even if I didn't have the logic to back up my choice

e) YES, always! I was the most sensitive kid in my class and felt like an old soul the whole time during my school years!

16. You listen to what your gut is trying to tell you even if it doesn't seem logical/practical at the moment. Later on, it turns out to be true.

a) Nah, don't think I'll get it right even if I do try it

b) I've done this once but haven't dared to do it ever again

c) Well, I follow my intuition but sometimes I have to rely on facts

d) Pretty much, though I did end up following logic a few times (and got it wrong)

e) There hasn't been one decision I've based on my gut that I ended up regretting later.

17. You feel content & happy with the life you're living. You don't feel like something's missing.

a) I'm working on being a bit more content, but I don't know where to look for guidance.

b) Rarely, I have my doubts almost daily

c) Some days I do, some days I don't—don't we all?

d) On most days I'm pretty happy, though the occasional bad day happens

e) Yup, yup, that's me!

18. You feel confident and know how to act even in the most unexpected situations or events.

a) Fear & panic paralyze me instantly if something unexpected happens

b) I want to say I do but haven't really been in a situation like that recently

c) I try to, and if in doubt, I turn to my gut for further guidance

d) Quite often I do! I also don't get easily panicked or scared

e) Always, and I know my intuition will help me find a solution to whatever problem I encounter.

19. You can hear what your gut is trying to tell you.

a) I wouldn't be able to hear even if I tried to.

b) When something's really important, urgent, yup!

c) Well, sometimes I can but it's not always clear as what I'd like it to be

d) I've rarely had a moment of doubt while listening to my gut

e) Yeah, and almost all of my decisions (big or small) are based on gut feelings!

20. You meditate and you spend a lot of time developing your EQ.

a) Why would I do that? Oh, and you can develop your EQ?

b) No, but I'd like to start

c) Well, I try to be consistent with my meditation but can't get 7 out of 7 days a week. I'm trying though!

d) Yes, on most days I work quite a bit on my self-development

e) Of course, I do this daily, without any excuses!

Once done answering the questions, add up the score as shown below:

Each a) scores 0

Each b) scores 1

Each c) scores 2

Each d) scores 3

Each e) scores 4

RESULTS: MAXIMUM SCORE
OF 80 POINTS

Level 1: less than 12 points

You're probably the most rational among your group of friends. You don't feel like you have a sixth sense—neither do you feel the need to.

You probably base most of your decisions on logic and hardcore facts. Even if something's fishy, you lightly brush it off and decide to follow what your brain is telling you instead. If you want to get the most out of your intuition, then you may need to learn how to listen to your intuition more closely.

Level 2: 13 – 35 points

Your intuition is pretty much basic. But hey, that's not that bad! Most of the people have their intuition at this level. That means that your intuition will kick in as an instinct whenever you need it the most—in a survival situation, let's say.

Right now, your intuition is that little voice at the back of your mind that tells you not to go down the dark alley or not to board the plane that turned out to crash because you got distracted on the phone. Believe it or not, it's often the little choices like that that have saved the lives of thousands of people! Other than that, you don't rely on intuition daily and you prefer to look at the facts in front of you. If you decide to work on developing your intuition closely, you might notice that you'd be able to make better decisions regarding your life's purpose.

Level 3: 36 – 51 points

Your intuition is strong enough to allow you to sense what the people around you are feeling or thinking. You're a very good judge of character, but also very emphatic. That allows you to be a great leader for others—people seem to easily trust you and like you!

You have no trouble getting a hold of other people's feelings or moods, and friends probably adore you for your ability to cheer them up when they're feeling down. Whenever people close to you are experiencing trouble, you're able to easily tell something's going on.

You also tend to make good decisions—or at least, you can sense trouble. If you continue working on your intuition, you may learn how to harness and use its power to help you thrive in other areas of your life, such as building a stronger career or becoming a thought leader in your area of expertise.

Level 4: 52 - 70

The intuition you possess sparks up your creativity and allows you to create things that no one ever thought about making before. You very likely work on your own and are a born visionary—an artist, an entrepreneur, someone who's ready to take on the world and lead by example.

You know what your true purpose is and you have the vision to help you achieve it. You're probably very charismatic and people often like you and trust you without you even doing much—it's your energy that attracts them to you!

Sometimes, the everyday clutter clouds your mind and hinders your decision-making process which, most of the time, is based on what your gut is telling you! However, after taking some time alone, you're usually able to reconnect to your true self and continue working on your higher purpose.

Level 5: 71 – 80

If your intuition is developed at this level, then you've done an awesome job with yourself! The subconscious, unconscious, and conscious parts of your mind are all working together to help you make the most out of every situation you get in.

You always listen to your intuition, even when logic and facts point in the other direction. So far, your intuition has never failed you!

You're also excelling at decision-making under pressure because somehow you always make the right decision at the right time! You never get stuck with the wrong people nor surround yourself with people that you & your body don't like. By now, you're probably aware of your divine purpose and how you can help make the world a better place. You meditate daily and you are looking to inspire others to do the same.

REFERENCES

CHAPTER 4

- Kahneman, D. (2011). *Thinking, fast and slow.* London: Penguin.

CHAPTER 5

- Dreyfus, E. (2013). Right brain, left brain |. Retrieved from http://docdreyfus.com/psychologically-speaking/right-brain-left-brain/

- Bergland, C. (2017). The Microbiome-Gut-Brain Axis Relies on Your Vagus Nerve. Retrieved from https://www.psychologytoday.com/us/blog/the-athletes-way/201708/the-microbiome-gut-brain-axis-relies-your-vagus-nerve

- Head, C. (2017). intuitive thinking | dr carol head. Retrieved from https://drcarolhead.com.au/tag/intuitive-thinking/

CHAPTER 6

- Marcus, B. (2015). Intuiton Is An Essential Leadership Tool. Retrieved from https://www.forbes.com/sites/bonniemarcus/2015/09/01/intuiton-is-an-essential-leadership-tool/#3ced6d7d1c18

- How Do Healthcare Providers Use Intuition? | Taking Charge of Your Health & Wellbeing. (n.d.) Retrieved from https://www.takingcharge.csh.umn.edu/explore-healing-practices/intuition-healthcare/how-do-healthcare-providers-use-intuition

CHAPTER 8

- Opashinov, K. (2009). Top Six Basic Intuition Questions - Vitality Magazine. Retrieved from http://vitalitymagazine.com/article/top-six-basic-intuition-questions/

CHAPTER 9

- Chopra, D. (2010). Ask Deepak: How to Trust Your Intuition. Retrieved from http://www.oprah.com/spirit/lacking-intuition-ask-deepak

- Flora, C. (2007). Gut Almighty. Retrieved from https://www.psychologytoday.com/us/articles/200705/gut-almighty

CHAPTER 10

- Durgananda, S. *Meditation, Subconscious Mind and Intuition.* (n.d.) Retrieved from https://www.sivananda.eu/fileadmin/user_upload/inspiration/swami_durgananda/Meditation-Subconscious-Mind-and-Intuition.pdf

- Turner, A. (n.d.) How Meditation Changes Your Brain Frequency. Retrieved from https://www.mindbodygreen.com/0-12491/how-meditation-changes-your-brain-frequency.html

- Delta Brainwaves & Spirituality. Retrieved from http://drjoedispenza.com/files/understanding-brainwaves_white_paper.pdf

- Pilard, N. (2018). C. G. Jung and intuition: from the mindscape of the paranormal to the heart of psychology. *Journal Of Analytical Psychology, 63*(1), 65-84. doi: 10.1111/1468-5922.12380

- Robson, D. (2014). Psychology: The truth about the paranormal. Retrieved from http://www.bbc.com/future/story/20141030-the-truth-about-the-paranormal

Manufactured by Amazon.ca
Bolton, ON